HOW TO EAT CHOCOLATE

For Debbie, who met her
hero David Bowie in a lift
but couldn't talk to him
because she had a mouth
full of chocolate.

First published in the United Kingdom in 2023
by Skittledog, an imprint of Thames & Hudson Ltd,
181A High Holborn, London WC1V 7QX

Concept and layout © Thames & Hudson 2023

Text © Sarah Ford 2023
Illustrations © Kari Modén 2023

British Library Cataloguing-in-Publication Data
A catalogue record for this book is available
from the British Library

ISBN 978-1-83776-020-6

Printed and bound in China by C&C Printing Offset Co., Ltd

Be the first to know about our new releases,
exclusive content and author events by visiting
skittledog.com
thamesandhudson.com
thamesandhudsonusa.com
thamesandhudson.com.au

HOW TO
EAT
CHOCOLATE

SARAH FORD

Skittledog

Contents

How to Eat a Bar of Chocolate

A wise person once said, "A visit from a friend is nice, but a visit from a friend bearing chocolate is a delight." Chocolate has a way of making even the worst day bearable, and most people, if they could choose just three things to eat for the rest of their lives, would include chocolate. How to eat a bar of chocolate? Let me count the ways: delicious straight from the package, rich and unctuous cooked in a dessert, enticing baked in a cake, and tantalizing when surreptitiously added to a chili con carne to make it rich and glossy—no one would guess the secret ingredient, but they might wonder how it could taste so good. And chocolate given as a gift will never gather dust on a shelf—it is always welcome.

Where did it all start?

Chocolate has a long and rich history, but also a checkered one. This glorious gift from Mother Nature was enjoyed by the Olmecs in Mexico as early as 1750BCE, and by the Mayans and Aztecs. These ancient civilizations recognized its qualities— the beans were so valuable they were even used as currency. They produced a bitter chocolate drink made from the crushed beans mixed with spices, which would be unrecognizable to us today but was extremely popular among the wealthy at the time.

By the late 1500s, after the Spanish conquest of the Aztecs, chocolate was making its presence felt in Europe. It was first used as a bitter medicine, but as soon as the monks thought to sweeten it, its popularity took off. The high demand from European countries meant more and more plantations grew up in the colonies, all of which were worked by slaves.

It grows on trees!

Chocolate is made from the fruit of the cacao tree, which grows in tropical regions where the weather is humid. The cacao beans are harvested by hand using machetes, then the pods are split open and left to ferment in baskets. The fermentation process is important as this is when the flavor develops—the best quality chocolate comes from beans that have been fermented the longest. After fermentation, the beans have to be dried in the sun; they are spread and turned by hand. This can take a couple of weeks, during which the beans will turn from a light red brown to a dark brown. Once this process is complete, they are packed and shipped around the world to be made into chocolate.

From bean to bar

Once the beans arrive with the chocolate maker, they are roasted to intensify the flavor. The shells are crushed and removed, leaving the chocolate nibs. The nibs are ground and liquefied to separate the cocoa mass and cocoa butter. To make chocolate, cocoa butter, cocoa mass, sugar, and milk (for milk chocolate) are mixed together in different proportions, according to the type of chocolate being made. The mixture is heated and stirred for several days to make it smooth—this process is called "conching." The mixture is then tempered (cooled and stirred), to form couverture. At this point, flavorings and other ingredients can be added, and after that the chocolate is ready for wrapping and packing.

Why choose Fairtrade?

Chocolate is produced all around the world by thousands of smallholders. By purchasing a bar of Fairtrade chocolate, you are guaranteeing that the farmers and those at the bottom of the supply chain receive a fair price for their produce. Consultation between workers and traders ensures that they earn enough to cover the cost of growing the crop. However, the cocoa farmers don't benefit from the price of the whole bar, so it is sensible to look beyond the Fairtrade mark and buy ethical brands which go even further. These days there is plenty of choice, so you can enjoy your chocolate secure in the knowledge that everyone in the process has been treated fairly. While there is still much to do, we have come a long way from the days when cocoa was farmed by slaves and eaten only by the rich.

Chocolate—to infinity and beyond

Although the chocolate bar has remained largely the same for hundreds of years, many companies are taking this basic foundation to new heights. Now is a great time for chocolate, with artisan makers coming up with new flavors and creations all the time, working more ethically with individual farmers to produce delicious variations. The humble bar of chocolate has only just started its exciting journey. And for us, this means that there are ever more ways to eat it. This book touches upon the many great things you can do with a bar of chocolate—games, syrups, cocktails, hacks, and more to keep any chocolate lover endlessly occupied and their cravings ultimately satisfied. This book and a simple bar of chocolate—what more could anyone ask?

Recipe Notes

This book includes recipes made with nuts and nut derivatives. Anyone who has allergic reactions to nuts or nut derivatives, or who is vulnerable to allergies, is advised to avoid dishes made with nuts or nut derivatives.

For reliable results in the baking recipes, use the weight measurements supplied rather than cup measurements.

Standard level spoon measurements are used:
- 1 tablespoon = 15ml
- 1 dessertspoon = 10ml
- 1 teaspoon = 5ml

Coffee: 1 shot = 2 tablespoons (30ml).

Ovens should be preheated to the specified temperature. For fan ovens, follow the manufacturer's instructions to adjust the time and temperature.

Melt

Boozy Chocolate Sauce

Pour over chocolate cake or a dessert of your choice, and serve with ice cream. Coffee, almond, and orange liqueurs all work well here, as does brandy.

– 2 tablespoons butter
– ½ cup (125ml) heavy cream
– 1 tablespoon superfine sugar
– 1 tablespoon liqueur or spirit (optional)
– 2 tablespoons semi-sweet chocolate, melted (see page 20)

Place the butter, cream, sugar, and liqueur in a saucepan over a low heat and stir until combined. Remove from the heat and stir into the melted chocolate. Serve warm or cold.

Shiny Chocolate Sauce Glossy and delicious. Try drizzling it over poached pears or cheesecake.

- ⅔ cup (125g) superfine sugar
- ½ cup (125ml) water
- ⅔ cup (200g) semi-sweet chocolate, melted (see page 20)
- 2 tablespoons butter

Place the sugar and water in a saucepan over a low heat and stir until the sugar has dissolved. Increase the heat and boil for 1 minute, then remove from the heat and allow to cool for 1 minute. Add the melted chocolate and butter and stir until the sauce is shiny. Gently reheat if you want to serve it warm.

Milk Chocolate Dipping & Drizzling Sauce
Rich and creamy, perfect served with fruit, pretzels, cookies, or breadsticks for dipping.

- 1 cup + 2 tablespoons (200g) milk chocolate, chopped
- ½ cup (125ml) heavy cream
- 2 tablespoons dark corn syrup
- 3 tablespoons butter

Melt the chocolate and cream in a bain marie (see page 20), stirring until the chocolate has melted and the mixture is smooth. Place the dark corn syrup and butter in a saucepan over a low heat and warm gently, stirring until mixed. Add the chocolate mixture and stir until smooth. Serve warm or cold.

Easy White Chocolate Sauce
A simple sauce, delicious with just about any dessert—try it drizzled over ice cream, apple tart, or ginger cake.

- 1 cup (175g) white chocolate, chopped
- ⅓ cup (75ml) whipping cream

Place the chocolate and cream in a saucepan over a low heat and warm gently. Stir until the chocolate has melted and the sauce is smooth. Serve warm or cold.

Chocolate Syrup
A much lighter, shinier sauce, ideal for cocktails, coffees, milkshakes, or drizzling on ice cream.

- ¾ cup (150g) superfine sugar
- 1 cup (240ml) water
- ½ cup (50g) cocoa powder
- pinch of salt
- 2 teaspoons vanilla extract
- 1 tablespoon semi-sweet chocolate, chopped

Place the sugar and water in a saucepan over a low heat and stir until the sugar has dissolved. Remove from the heat and whisk in the cocoa powder and salt. Add the vanilla and semi-sweet chocolate and gently reheat, stirring until the chocolate has melted and the syrup is shiny. Store in the refrigerator for up to two weeks.

Cheat's Chocolate Pudding

Warm a 14-ounce (400g) can of pudding in a saucepan over a medium heat. Add ½ cup (100g) of chopped semi-sweet chocolate and stir once. Wait until the chocolate has melted then serve as marbled pudding or stir well to make chocolate pudding.

Drizzling Chocolate

Drizzling chocolate over shop-bought or homemade cookies, sheet cakes, or cakes is an easy way to take the deliciousness to a whole new level. Try milk, white, or semi-sweet chocolate or a mixture of all three. Simply melt the chocolate in a microwave or bain marie until smooth (see page 20). Place your bakes on a cookie sheet lined with nonstick parchment paper and use a fork or teaspoon to drizzle the melted chocolate back and forth over the top. For a neater result, try using a pastry bag. Work quickly before the chocolate starts to cool and set.

Chocolate Cream Cheese Frosting

This is a delicious topping for a chocolate cake and a little healthier than buttercream icing. Team it with raspberry preserves for extra deliciousness.

MAKES ENOUGH
FOR 1 LARGE CAKE

- 1⅓ cup (350g) cream cheese
- 1⅓ cup (175g) confectioners' sugar, sieved
- ½ cup + 2 tablespoons (175g) milk chocolate, melted (see page 20)

Place the cream cheese in a mixing bowl and beat with a fork to soften, then slowly add the confectioners' sugar. Allow the chocolate to cool a little, then stir into the frosting mixture until glossy.

Milk Chocolate Buttercream
A good general frosting for cakes, cupcakes, and cookies. You can also use it to sandwich together cakes and cookies—or enjoy it straight from the bowl!

MAKES ENOUGH
FOR 1 LARGE CAKE

- ½ cup (100g) butter
- 1⅔ cup (200g) confectioners' sugar
- 2 tablespoons milk or semi-sweet chocolate, melted (see page 20)
- dash of vanilla extract
- dash of milk, to loosen (optional)

Beat the butter and confectioners' sugar together in a mixing bowl until fluffy. Allow the chocolate to cool a little, then beat into the frosting until it is soft and spreadable. Add the vanilla and a little milk if it is too stiff. Any leftover buttercream can be stored in the refrigerator for up to two weeks.

White Chocolate Buttercream

Simply use white chocolate instead of milk or semi-sweet chocolate. This frosting is delicious as a filling for a simple sponge cake with lashings of blackberry or blackcurrant preserves.

How to Melt Chocolate

The best ways to melt chocolate are by using a microwave or a bain marie. The microwave method is simplest as it is quicker and less messy, but it can be a bit more difficult to get just right. Chocolate melts faster if it contains more cocoa butter, so semi-sweet chocolate will melt the fastest. Milk and white chocolate contain more sugar and can burn easily, so it's important to keep checking and stirring—they will also have a thicker consistency when melted.

In a microwave

Break your chocolate into even-sized pieces and place in a plastic pitcher or bowl. Turn the microwave to a low power and give the chocolate a 20-second blast then mix well. Once the chocolate is starting to melt, microwave for 5 or 10 seconds at a time, stirring well between blasts, and stop before the chocolate has fully melted as stirring will finish it off. The chocolate should still be cool to touch.

In a bain marie

This is the best method for controlling the melting of your chocolate, but it can take a little longer. Pour 2 inches (5cm) of water into a small saucepan and heat until it is gently simmering. Place a heat-safe bowl on top of the pan, making sure the base of the bowl does not touch the water. Place the chocolate pieces in the bowl and let them melt, stirring regularly. Remove the bowl from the pan and allow the chocolate to cool a little while stirring.

Mmmm Mocha A sophisticated alternative to hot chocolate.

SERVES 1

- 1 tablespoon semi-sweet chocolate, grated
- 2-3 teaspoons hot chocolate powder, to taste
- 1 double shot of espresso coffee
- hot whole milk, to top up
- whipped cream (optional)
- mini marshmallows (optional)

Place the chocolate in a mug and melt in a microwave until smooth (see page 20). Add the hot chocolate powder and espresso and mix thoroughly. Top up with hot milk, stir well, and top with whipped cream and marshmallows if you are feeling decadent.

Banoccy Breakfast Smoothie This will keep you happy until lunchtime.

SERVES 1-2

- 1 banana, broken into pieces
- 1 tablespoon semi-sweet chocolate, melted (see page 20)
- 1 dessertspoon almond butter
- 1 dessertspoon chocolate-flavored pea protein powder
- 1 cup (240ml) almond or oat milk
- 1 tablespoon rolled oats (optional)

Place all the ingredients in a blender and blitz until smooth.

Art

Decorating Cookies

There are many simple ways to decorate cookies using chocolate. Decorate shop-bought cookies to make them extra special, or make the Chocolate Sugar Cookies on page 82. It is important that your cookies have cooled down before you start decorating.

- ⅔ cup (200g) white chocolate, melted (see page 20)
- ⅔ cup (200g) milk chocolate, melted (see page 20)
- 20 cookies
- chopped nuts, sprinkles, or other toppings

You will also need:
- 2 pastry bags fitted with fine nozzles
- nonstick parchment paper
- wire rack

Fill the pastry bags with the two different types of melted chocolate and practice piping on a piece of nonstick parchment paper before you begin.

To cover the top of a cookie with chocolate, start by piping a neat border around the edges and leave to cool for a moment. Then fill in the center using the pastry bag or by simply spooning on the chocolate so that it runs up to the border, without the fear of it dripping over the edges of the cookie.

Alternatively, place the melted chocolates in separate bowls and half-dip the cookies. This can get messy, so it is a good idea to have a wire rack standing on a sheet of nonstick parchment paper ready to take the cookies after dipping.

Before the chocolate sets, top the cookies with chopped nuts or sprinkles.

Brushstroke Feathers

These simple and stylish nature-inspired cake toppers, and those on the following pages, take cakes and cupcakes to a whole new level. Chocolate feathers are the perfect topping for a special cake, adding real glamour. Cover the top and sides of your cake with chocolate buttercream (see page 19) and arrange the white, milk, and semi-sweet chocolate feathers around it.

MAKES ABOUT
30 FEATHERS

- ⅓ cup (100g) white chocolate, melted (see page 20)
- ⅓ cup (100g) milk chocolate, melted (see page 20)
- ⅓ cup (100g) semi-sweet chocolate, melted (see page 20)

You will also need:
- nonstick parchment paper
- 3 paint brushes, about 1½ inches (4cm) across with rounded edges (you can trim the bristles to round the edges)

Pour a teaspoon of melted chocolate onto a sheet of parchment paper—the diameter of your chocolate puddle should be just wider than your brush. Position the brush on the chocolate near the left-hand side of the puddle then draw it to the right across the puddle and keep going to create a feather shape in a single stroke. The chocolate needs to be thin, but not so thin you can see the paper through it. Work quickly to make plenty of different-sized feathers from your three different types of chocolate, as inevitably some will break. Cool the feathers in the refrigerator for 20 minutes or until set.

Once your feathers have set, peel them off the parchment paper and stick them into the top of the cake, or around the sides. They are fragile and will melt easily, so make sure you have cool hands and handle with care. Any unused feathers can be stored in an airtight container in the refrigerator for two weeks and used to decorate cupcakes or hot chocolate.

Elegant Butterflies

These beautiful toppers might take a little practice to perfect, but they are well worth the effort.

- ⅓ cup (100g) white chocolate, melted (see page 20)
- ⅓ cup (100g) semi-sweet chocolate, melted (see page 20)

You will also need:
- thin black marker pen
- nonstick parchment paper
- 3 pastry bags fitted with fine nozzles

Use a marker pen to draw or trace plenty of different butterfly shapes on the non-waxed side of the parchment paper. Cut them out very roughly, leaving a good border of paper round the edges of each. Place the melted chocolate in the three different pastry bags and practice piping thin, even lines before you start your butterflies.

Gently fold each paper butterfly in half, waxed sides together, so that the wings are on either side of the fold. Open a hardback book flat on the work surface and put the fold of your butterfly between the open pages, waxed side up. Gently pipe the chocolate over the traced design—the book should support the wings in a curved, upright position. Repeat to make butterflies of different colors. If you find this too fiddly, try piping on a flat surface instead. Cool the butterflies in the refrigerator for 20 minutes or until set, then arrange on top of your cake. Leftover butterflies can be stored in an airtight container in the refrigerator for two weeks.

Herby Chocolate Leaves

Any leaves can be used to imprint the chocolate, but those with prominent veins such as basil, mint, bay, or rose are most successful. Make sure the leaves are clean and avoid poisonous plants.

– 24 fresh leaves
– ⅔ cup (200g) milk or
  semi-sweet chocolate,
  melted (see page 20)

You will also need:
– small pastry brush or
  paint brush
– nonstick parchment paper
– toothpick

Wash and thoroughly dry your leaves, then lay them face down on the parchment paper so the veins are facing upwards. Gently paint the leaves with the chocolate, stopping short of the edges. Make sure you don't get any chocolate on the undersides, as this will make it difficult to peel the leaves off. Allow the chocolate to harden in the refrigerator for approximately 20 minutes.

Repeat the painting process to add a second layer of chocolate, then cool again. Once the chocolate has set, quickly and gently peel off the leaves, starting at the stems. Use a toothpick to accentuate the veins in the chocolate if they are not clear. Any leftover leaves can be stored in an airtight container in the refrigerator for two weeks.

Christmas Trees

These are simple to make and give a festive vibe to cookies, cupcakes, and other Christmas treats. It is easy to create your own designs. Make plenty of different-sized trees as they are fragile and can break or melt easily.

– ⅔ cup (200g) milk, white, or semi-sweet chocolate, melted (see page 20)

You will also need:
– thin black marker pen
– nonstick parchment paper
– pastry bag fitted with a fine nozzle

Draw your tree designs on the non-waxed side of the parchment paper, then turn over the paper, waxed side up. Place the melted chocolate in the pastry bag and carefully pipe over the tree designs. Make sure your piping is continuous and not too thin to avoid breakages when you peel off the paper. Allow the trees to cool in the refrigerator for approximately 20 minutes, then peel them off the paper. Decorate your sweet treats with frosting and arrange the chocolate trees on top. Any leftover trees can be stored in an airtight container in the refrigerator for two weeks.

Painted Peanut Butter Cups

Nutty mouthfuls, perfect with a cup of coffee.

MAKES 15-20

- ⅔ cup (200g) semi-sweet chocolate, melted (see page 20)
- ½ cup (125g) creamy peanut butter
- 2½ tablespoons maple syrup

You will also need:
- mini silicone cup mold or mini paper baking cups
- small pastry brush or paint brush

Paint the insides of the cups with the melted chocolate, then allow the chocolate to harden in the refrigerator for approximately 20 minutes. Repeat the painting and cooling process to add two more layers of chocolate to build up the chocolate shells, then allow the finished shells to cool for another 20 minutes in the refrigerator.

Mix the peanut butter and maple syrup together and use the mixture to fill the cases, leaving a small gap at the top for a chocolate topping. Spoon melted chocolate over the top of the peanut butter to seal the cases. Freeze for approximately 30 minutes, then remove from the cups and allow to come to room temperature before serving.

Bubble Wrap Cake Decoration

The perfect decoration for a delicious homemade chocolate cake. Add some luscious fresh berries for texture and color.

– ⅔ cup (200g) milk
  chocolate, melted
  (see page 20)

You will also need:
– bubble wrap
– pastry brush

Lay the bubble wrap out flat on a work surface, bubble side up. Paint the melted chocolate thickly over the bubble wrap, then allow to cool in the refrigerator for approximately 15 minutes—the chocolate should be firm but still a little flexible. Peel off the chocolate, break it into uneven pieces, and use it to decorate your cake.

Jazzy Chocolate Pretzels
These pretzels are deliciously salty and sweet, and fun for anyone from two to a hundred years old! Place all the ingredients in little bowls and let everyone decorate the pretzels. It's bound to get messy, so choose a wipe-clean surface.

– 1 large package of salted pretzels
– ⅓ cup (100g) white chocolate, melted (see page 20)
– ⅓ cup (100g) milk chocolate, melted (see page 20)
– ⅓ cup (100g) semi-sweet chocolate, melted (see page 20)
– selection of toppings, such as dried raspberry pieces, colored sprinkles, desiccated coconut, fine pink rock salt, colored icing for drizzling, edible glitter

You will also need:
– nonstick parchment paper

Dip the pretzels in the melted chocolate or drizzle them with chocolate using a teaspoon, then place them on a sheet of parchment paper. Before the chocolate starts to set, sprinkle the pretzels with your toppings. When finished, leave the chocolate to set for 20 minutes.

How to Curl, Swirl, & Grate Your Bar

These decorative techniques look impressive but will only take a few minutes of your time.

Chocolate curls

Use a vegetable peeler to pare chocolate curls from the side of a bar of chocolate—the thickness of the bar will determine how big your curls are. If the curls are breaking up, soften the bar very briefly in a microwave set to defrost.

For more professional curls, spread a thick layer of melted chocolate on a chopping board and leave to set in the refrigerator. Once hard, scrape a knife angled on its side across the chocolate to create long thin curls, known as "caraque." Use your chocolate curls to decorate iced cakes, desserts, and drinks.

Grated chocolate

A sprinkling of grated chocolate on cold desserts and drinks adds a touch of luxury and makes them extra delicious. Use a coarse grater—if the chocolate is hard to grate, soften the bar very briefly in a microwave set to defrost.

Send a message with chocolate

If you are having a party, pipe your guests' names or messages on the dessert plates. This can be done well in advance to give you time to perfect it and allow the chocolate to set. Simply spoon melted semi-sweet chocolate (see page 20) into a small pastry bag fitted with a fine nozzle. Practice writing your guests' names on paper before tackling the plates. Alternatively, you can pipe your message on nonstick parchment paper, allow it to set in the refrigerator, then gently peel off the paper and use the chocolate words to decorate a dessert or cake.

Celebrate

White Modeling Chocolate

Just like firm Play-Doh, but much more delicious! Use your modeling chocolate to make decorations and figures for cakes, or roll it out to cover a cake or to cut out shapes or letters. You can store it in the refrigerator, but allow it to soften at room temperature before using.

– 1⅓ cups (400g) white chocolate, melted (see page 20)
– 3½ tablespoons dark corn syrup, warmed

You will also need:
– plastic wrap

When the melted chocolate and syrup are just warm, stir them together in a large bowl. Keep stirring until the mixture comes away from the sides of the bowl. Lay a large sheet of plastic wrap out on a work surface, then spread the mixture on top using a palette knife until it is ½–¾ inch (1–2cm) thick. Wrap the modeling chocolate in the plastic wrap, then wrap in another sheet of plastic wrap. Leave it to set at room temperature for 24 hours or, if you need it quickly, cool it in a refrigerator for 2 hours or until firm.

Colored modeling chocolate

Simply add food coloring to the cooled melted chocolate before you add the syrup. Add a little bit at a time and keep stirring until you get the desired color.

Modeling chocolate tips

- Modeling chocolate can be stored for months in a refrigerator. Keep it wrapped in plastic wrap and place it in an airtight bag or box. To use, break off bits and warm and mold in your hands.

- Keep it away from water as it will ruin the chocolate and make it unusable.

- If it becomes too hard, warm slowly and gently for a few seconds in a microwave set to defrost.

- When rolling it out, dust the work surface and rolling pin with confectioners' sugar to prevent sticking.

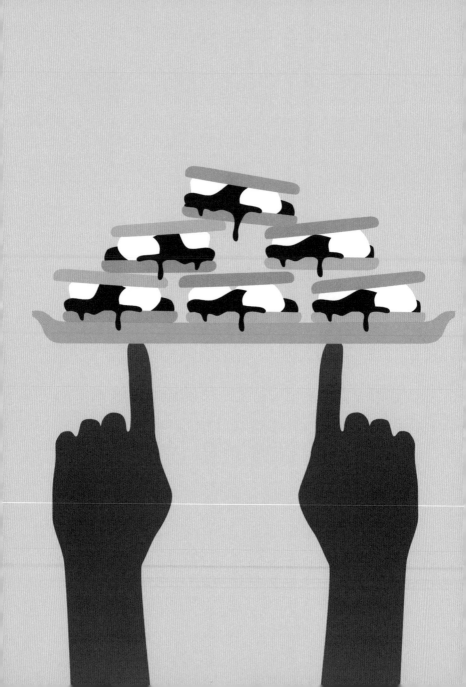

S'mores Indoors

This is the lazy way to make s'mores, whatever the weather. These are a real crowd pleaser and perfect for a party—they'll be ready in minutes.

MAKES 8

- 16 graham crackers
- 16 squares of milk chocolate, halved
- 16 marshmallows, halved

Place eight crackers face down on a cookie sheet and arrange four pieces of chocolate and four pieces of marshmallow on each. Make a flower pattern, alternating the chocolate and marshmallow pieces and getting them as close to the center of the cracker as possible as they will spread as they melt.

Place the tray under a preheated grill and cook until the marshmallows are soft and golden and the chocolate is starting to melt. Remove from the heat and top each with a second cracker, face up. Squish down and cool for a couple of minutes before tucking in to avoid burned mouths.

Simple Chocolate Flower Bowls

These easy-to-make chocolate bowls are great for serving ice cream at parties.

MAKES 12

- 1⅓ cups (400g)
  semi-sweet chocolate,
  melted (see page 20)
- ice cream and toppings,
  to serve

You will also need:

- 12 squares of nonstick
  parchment paper, about
  6 inches (15cm) across
- 12-hole muffin tray
- double-sided sticky tape
- pastry brush or paint brush

Press the parchment paper squares into the muffin tray so that they look like opening flowers, securing them underneath using a small piece of tape. One at a time, pour a dessertspoon of chocolate into each hole and paint it liberally up the sides of the paper to form petals. Allow the chocolate to harden in the refrigerator for approximately 20 minutes.

Repeat the painting and cooling process to add two more layers of chocolate to build up the chocolate bowls, then allow the finished bowls to cool for another 20–30 minutes in the refrigerator until hard. Carefully peel off the paper and place the flower bowls in the refrigerator until you are ready to serve, filled with ice cream and toppings.

White Chocolate & Blueberry Cheat Cheesecakes
Quick and delightful, these little makeshift cheesecakes are made in minutes with no cooking involved. Top them with blueberries and you're ready to go.

MAKES 20

- 1½ cups (200g) white chocolate, grated
- ¾ cup (200g) cream cheese
- ½ cup (50g) confectioners' sugar, sieved
- dash of vanilla extract
- ⅔ cup (150ml) heavy cream
- 20 graham crackers
- blueberries, to decorate

Beat the chocolate, cream cheese, sugar, vanilla, and cream together in a mixing bowl until smooth. Chill in the refrigerator until ready to serve.

Spread the mixture thickly on the crackers, then top with blueberries and a sprinkle of confectioners' sugar.

Chocolate Butter
This is possibly the best thing ever! Beat ½ cup (125g) of salted butter at room temperature in a mixing bowl until smooth. Add ⅓ cup (125g) of melted and cooled semi-sweet chocolate, then sieve in a dessertspoon of cocoa powder and mix well. Transfer to a serving dish and chill in the refrigerator until needed. This butter is absolutely delicious on toast or hot pancakes.

Chocolate Pancakes
Fluffy and chocolaty—the perfect celebration breakfast for a birthday. Serve them hot with maple syrup, chocolate sauce of your choice (see pages 12–15), or Chocolate Butter (see page 49).

(see pages 12–15), or Chocolate Butter (see page 49).

MAKES 10-12

– 1½ cups (200g) self-rising flour
– 1 teaspoon baking powder
– pinch of salt
– 1 tablespoon superfine sugar
– 2 eggs, beaten
– 1¼ cups (300ml) milk
– ¾ cup (125g) milk chocolate, finely chopped
– butter, for frying

Sieve the flour, baking powder, and salt into a large mixing bowl and stir in the sugar. Place the beaten eggs and milk in a pitcher and whisk to combine. Make a well in the center of the dry ingredients and add the egg mixture. Whisk well to make the pancake batter–don't worry if there are a few lumps. Add the chocolate and fold into the batter, then allow it to stand for 15 minutes.

Melt a knob of butter in a skillet over a medium heat and tilt the pan so the butter coats the surface. Make four puddles of batter in the pan, 2-3 tablespoons of batter per pancake. Cook for about 2 minutes until the batter starts to bubble, then flip over and cook the other sides for 2 minutes more, or until golden and fluffy. Remove from the skillet and keep warm in a low oven while you make the remaining pancakes. Serve immediately.

The Chocolate Game

You will need:
- 6-12 players
- 1 large bar of milk chocolate
- dinner plate
- knife and fork
- woolly hat
- woolly mittens
- woolly scarf
- 2 dice

Sit everyone in a circle and place the wrapped chocolate on the plate, the knife and fork, and the dress-up things in the center. Each person takes a turn to throw the dice, then passes them to the player on their left. The first person to throw a double number has to dress up in the hat, mittens, and scarf, unwrap the chocolate, and start trying to eat it with the knife and fork. The other players continue to throw the dice in turn until someone else rolls a double, at which point they swap with the other player, dress up, and eat as much chocolate as they can until the next double.

Face Race

You will need:
- 2-4 players
- 2-4 chairs
- 1 large bar of milk chocolate, broken into squares

Each player sits on a chair and tilts their head backwards. A square of chocolate is placed on their forehead. The aim is to get the chocolate into their mouth without using their hands and eat it as quickly as possible. The winner is the first to swallow.

Feed a Friend

You will need:
- 2 players
- 2 chairs
- 2 blindfolds
- 2 wooden spoons
- 2 bowls
- 1 large bar of milk chocolate, broken into squares

The players should sit on chairs, facing each other and wearing blindfolds. Each player is given a wooden spoon and a bowl of chocolate squares. The object of the game is for the players to use the wooden spoons to feed each other as many chocolate squares as possible in 60 seconds. They cannot touch the chocolate with their hands. Only the pieces that make it into the mouth count. The winner is the one who feeds the most chocolate to their friend.

White Chocolate Raspberry Frappe

Serve at an elegant tea party or as a dessert after a dinner party. Instead of raspberries, you could try mango, strawberries, or blueberries.

SERVES 1

– ⅔ cup (150ml) milk
– ⅓ cup (50g) white chocolate, grated
– large handful of raspberries, plus extra to decorate
– 1 scoop of vanilla ice cream
– 2-3 crushed ice cubes

Place all the ingredients in a blender and blitz for 10-15 seconds. Serve in a tall glass, decorated with raspberries.

The Sass
This sweet cocktail is like Black Forest gateau in a glass. Perfect at the end of a meal.

SERVES 1

– 2 tablespoons cherry brandy
– 2 tablespoons Chocolate Syrup (see page 15)
– 2 tablespoons half and half
– 4 pitted cherries
– ice, to serve
– 1 cherry, to decorate

Blitz all of the ingredients together in a blender until smooth then pour into a cocktail glass over ice. Pop a cherry on top to decorate.

Creamy Mocha Martini A rich and creamy cocktail that is perfect for lovers of chocolate and coffee.

- ⅓ cup (50g) semi-
  sweet chocolate,
  melted (see page 20)
- handful of ice cubes
- ⅓ cup + 2 tablespoons
  (100ml) chocolate liqueur
- ⅓ cup + 2 tablespoons
  (100ml) Irish coffee
  cream liqueur
- ⅓ cup + 2 tablespoons
  (100ml) vodka
- grated chocolate,
  to decorate

Dip the rims of two chilled martini glasses into the melted chocolate, then drizzle the leftover chocolate into the glasses to make a scribble pattern. Add the ice, liqueurs, and vodka to a cocktail shaker and shake until a frost forms on the outside of the shaker. Strain the cocktail into the glasses and serve decorated with a sprinkle of grated chocolate on top.

Ultimate Chocolate Milkshake

This shake is thick and creamy, like you'd find in a diner. You can experiment by adding other ingredients, such as peanut butter or banana instead of the chocolate ice cream. For a boozy version, try adding a shot of bourbon.

SERVES 1

– 1 tablespoon Chocolate Syrup (see page 15), plus extra to serve
– 2 small scoops of chocolate ice cream
– ⅔ cup (150ml) milk
– whipped cream, to serve

Blitz all the ingredients in a blender for 10–15 seconds, or until thick and creamy. Serve topped with whipped cream and a drizzle of chocolate syrup.

Eggs-presso

This is a perfect morning pick-me-up after Easter. Place a leftover hollow chocolate egg in a coffee cup and drip two shots of hot espresso coffee over the top. Alternatively, stand the egg in an espresso cup like a boiled egg, cut the top off the egg and drip espresso into it. Eat by slurping with a small spoon.

Chocolate Straws

Take a chocolate-covered wafer bar, nibble the chocolate off both ends, dip it into your tea, coffee, or hot chocolate, and suck. Hey presto, a chocolate straw! Make sure you're not wearing a good shirt as it can get messy.

Sweet

Mini Fondues

These little pots of loveliness are just as suited to a formal dinner as a night in on the sofa. Serve the chocolate sauce in espresso cups nestled among the dippers on pretty plates.

SERVES 8

- ⅔ cup (150ml) whipping cream
- 1½ cups (250g) mixed semi-sweet and milk chocolate, chopped
- ¼ cup (50g) unsalted butter
- ½ teaspoon vanilla essence
- pinch of sea salt

To serve:
- breadsticks
- pretzels
- rice cakes
- salted potato chips
- cookies
- strawberries
- cherries
- pieces of mango
- pieces of banana
- marshmallows
- popcorn

Gently warm the cream and chocolate in a saucepan over a low heat, stirring until the chocolate has melted. Stir in the butter, vanilla, and salt. Serve warm in espresso cups with the dippers of your choice on the side.

Chocolate Coconut Bars

Moist, chewy, and coconutty in the center with a thick coating of creamy milk chocolate—what's not to like? They are very easy to make.

MAKES 12-15

- 2 cups (200g) desiccated coconut
- ¾ cup (200g) condensed milk
- 1 teaspoon vanilla extract
- ⅔ cup (200g) milk chocolate, melted (see page 20)

You will also need:
- cookie sheet
- nonstick parchment paper

Mix the coconut, condensed milk, and vanilla in a bowl then allow the mixture to stand for a couple of minutes to soften the coconut. Using your hands, shape the mixture into 12-15 small bars, about 3 x 1 inch (7 x 3cm). Place on a cookie sheet lined with nonstick parchment paper and chill in the refrigerator for an hour.

Once the bars are firm, transfer them to a wire rack standing on a sheet of parchment paper to catch the drips. Dip the bars into the melted chocolate until fully coated and return to the rack. Allow to set for 15 minutes, then return to the refrigerator until hard. Store in an airtight container in the refrigerator for up to two weeks.

Variation

To add a little magic, stir a couple of drops of pink or purple food coloring into the coconut mixture before forming the bars.

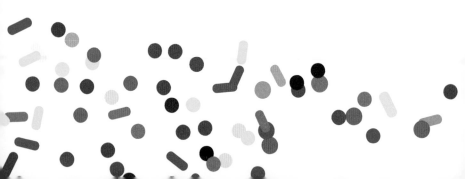

Snow Jazzies

Everyone can join in making these classic sweets. Use the best white chocolate you can find and choose your sprinkles according to the occasion. Red and green is perfect for Christmas—wrap them and tie with red ribbon for great stocking fillers.

MAKES ABOUT 60

– ⅔ cup (200g) white chocolate, melted (see page 20)
– ¼ cup (50g) sprinkles

You will also need:
– cookie sheet
– nonstick parchment paper

Line a cookie sheet with nonstick parchment paper and use a teaspoon to make small puddles of chocolate on the paper, gently shaping them into round disks. Before they start to set, top with the sprinkles. Chill in the refrigerator for 30 minutes, or until the chocolate has set. Peel off the paper and enjoy!

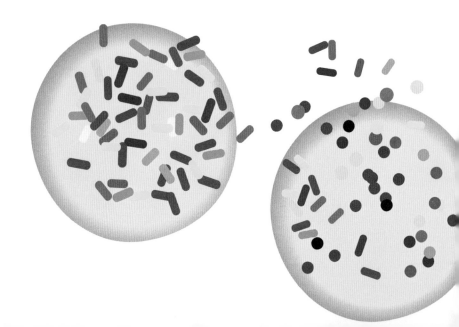

The Joy of Hot Chocolate

Comforting, decadent, simple joy in a mug, hot chocolate puts a smile on your face whatever the occasion.

Classic Hot Chocolate Creamy and indulgent, just how hot chocolate should be.

SERVES 2

– 1½ cups (350ml) whole milk
– ⅓ cup (100g) milk or semi-sweet chocolate, melted (see page 20)
– whipped cream
– mini marshmallows
– grated chocolate

Warm the milk in a small saucepan over a medium heat, taking care not to let it boil. Pour a little of the milk over the melted chocolate and stir well to loosen. Then transfer the chocolate mixture to the pan of milk and warm through while whisking. Serve in heat-safe glasses, topped with whipped cream, marshmallows, and grated chocolate.

Puerto Rican Cheesy Hot Chocolate

Place four or five small cubes of Edam cheese in a mug, then top up with hot chocolate. Use a spoon to enjoy the cheesy chocolate—don't knock it until you've tried it!

Boozy French Hot Chocolate

This classic recipe dates back over a hundred years and is made from the holy trinity—coffee, chocolate, and brandy. It would have originally been served sweet, but you can tailor the sugar to your taste.

SERVES 4

- 4 shots of espresso coffee
- 2 tablespoons semi-sweet chocolate, grated
- pinch of salt
- ⅓ cup + 2 tablespoons (100ml) brandy
- 600ml whole milk
- 4 teaspoons sugar, or to taste
- whipped cream, to serve

Place the coffee, chocolate, salt, and brandy in a small saucepan over a low heat and warm gently until the chocolate has melted. Slowly add the milk and bring to a simmer, whisking until smooth. Add the sugar, stir, and serve topped with whipped cream.

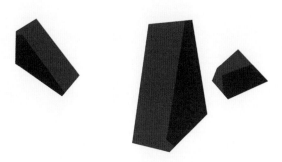

Unicorn Hot Chocolate

Sweet, creamy, and totally extra. More is more with this tribute to the unicorn—perfect for the young and the young at heart.

MAKES 2
MAGICAL DRINKS

– 1½ cups (350ml) milk
– 1 teaspoon vanilla extract
– ⅓ cup (100g) white chocolate, chopped
– whipped cream
– strawberry syrup
– pink mini marshmallows
– rainbow sprinkles

Gently warm the milk, vanilla, and white chocolate in a saucepan over a low heat until the chocolate has melted. Whisk until the mixture is smooth and warm. Serve in heat-safe glasses topped with whipped cream, syrup, marshmallows, and sprinkles.

Spiced Rum Truffles
These rich and delicious truffles make a great gift, if you don't eat them all first.

MAKES ABOUT 20

- ⅔ cup (150ml) heavy cream
- 1½ cups (250g) milk or semi-sweet chocolate, chopped
- 2 tablespoons butter, cubed
- 2 tablespoons spiced rum
- confectioners' sugar, to coat

Heat the cream to boiling point in a small saucepan over a low heat. Remove from the heat, add the chocolate and butter, and stir until melted and well mixed. Transfer to a bowl, add the rum, and mix until smooth. Chill in the refrigerator for 2 hours or overnight until the mixture is firm.

Sprinkle confectioners' sugar into a large bowl and use a teaspoon to scoop out walnut-sized pieces of the chocolate mixture into the bowl, a few at a time. Coat in the confectioners' sugar and roll into balls—it is important to have cool hands and to work quickly. Store the truffles in the refrigerator for up to a week—they will soften at room temperature.

Citrus Nut Truffles
A sweet treat to enjoy when you need a boost of protein—or just when you need a sweet treat.

MAKES ABOUT 30

- ½ cup (100g) soft dried apricots, roughly chopped
- ¾ cup (100g) hazelnuts, roughly chopped
- ½ cup (100g) dried cranberries
- finely grated zest of 1 orange
- 4 teaspoons orange liqueur
- ½ cup (150g) milk chocolate, melted (see page 20)
- confectioners' sugar, to coat

Blitz the apricots, nuts, cranberries, zest, and liqueur in a blender until finely chopped. Add the mixture to the melted chocolate and stir until well combined. Chill in the refrigerator for 30 minutes or until the mixture is firm.

Sprinkle confectioners' sugar into a large bowl and use a teaspoon to scoop out walnut-sized pieces of the chocolate mixture into the bowl, a few at a time. Coat in the confectioners' sugar and roll into balls. Store the truffles in the refrigerator for up to a week—they will soften at room temperature.

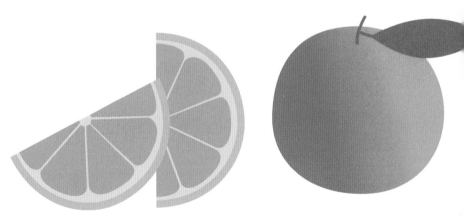

Almond Fudge
This creamy and nutty chocolate fudge is simple to make and requires no tricky boiling, just a little easy melting.

MAKES ABOUT
30 SQUARES

- 2 cups (350g) milk
  chocolate, chopped
- 1½ cups (400g)
  condensed milk
- 2 tablespoons
  unsalted butter
- 1 teaspoon vanilla extract
- 1 cup (150g) blanched
  almonds, finely chopped

You will also need:
- 9-inch (23cm) square
  brownie pan

Melt the chocolate, condensed milk, and butter in a bain marie (see page 20), stirring until smooth. Remove from the heat, add the vanilla and nuts, and stir well. Line a square pan with nonstick parchment paper, spoon the fudge mix into the tin and use a spatula to spread it out—it should be about 1 inch (2.5cm) thick. Chill in the refrigerator for several hours or preferably overnight, until firm. Cut the fudge into squares and store in the refrigerator for up to two weeks.

Minty Fudge
A white chocolate fudge with crunchy mint pieces.

MAKES ABOUT
30 SQUARES

- 2 cups (350g) white
  chocolate, chopped
- 1½ cups (400g)
  condensed milk
- 2 tablespoons
  unsalted butter
- ⅓ cup (40g) strong mint
  candies, finely chopped

You will also need:
- 9-inch (23cm) square
  brownie pan
- nonstick parchment paper

Melt the chocolate, condensed milk, and butter in a bain marie (see page 20), stirring until smooth. Remove from the heat, add the chopped candies, and stir well. Line a square pan with nonstick parchment paper, spoon the fudge mix into the tin and use a spatula to spread it out—it should be about 1 inch (2.5cm) thick. Chill in the refrigerator for several hours or preferably overnight, until firm. Cut the fudge into squares and store in the refrigerator for up to two weeks.

Choc Nut Spread

Perfect spread thickly on buttered toast, or serve it as a dip with pieces of fruit or breadsticks. If you want an extra kick, add a pinch of chili powder. The coconut oil will set when cooled, so you may need to warm the spread in the microwave for a few seconds before serving.

– 1 cup (125g) blanched hazelnuts
– ½ cup (150g) milk chocolate, melted (see page 20)
– 2 tablespoons semi-sweet chocolate, melted (see page 20)
– 1 dessertspoon cocoa powder
– 2 tablespoons coconut oil, melted
– 1 teaspoon vanilla extract
– 2 tablespoons maple syrup
– pinch of salt

Toast the hazelnuts in a dry skillet over a medium heat for about 1 minute or until they start to color.

Transfer the nuts to a blender and blitz until smooth. Add the remaining ingredients and blitz again until well mixed. Transfer to a sterilized jar and store in the refrigerator for up to a month.

Boozy Chocolate Cherries

Tip a punnet of cherries with their stalks into a bowl and pour in an alcohol of your choice until the cherries are just covered—brandy and amaretto liqueur work well. Leave the cherries to soak for several hours or overnight, then remove and dry the fruit. Place the leftover alcohol in the refrigerator to chill. Dip the cherries, one by one, into a bowl of melted semi-sweet chocolate (see page 20), covering just the fruit. Transfer them to a plate lined with nonstick parchment paper and chill in the refrigerator until the chocolate has set. Serve after dinner with a cup of coffee and a chilled shot of the steeped alcohol.

Strawberry Heart Popsicles

Remove the leaves and stalks from 10 large strawberries and slice each of them into three thick slices—they should resemble heart shapes. Arrange them on a tray lined with nonstick parchment paper and drizzle them with melted white chocolate (see page 20). Insert a toothpick into the point of each heart and freeze for 20 minutes before serving.

Chocolate Banana Ices

Peel five firm bananas and cut in half. Push popsicle sticks into the cut ends of the bananas and freeze for 15 minutes. Dip the frozen bananas into a bowl of melted milk chocolate (see page 20), then sprinkle them with chopped nuts, desiccated coconut, or rainbow sprinkles. Stand them upright in a popsicle stand and freeze for at least 1 hour before serving.

Overnight Oats

Make them the night before for the easiest breakfast ever.

SERVES 3-4

- 1 cup (75g) rolled oats
- 4 tablespoons coconut yogurt
- 1 tablespoon maple syrup, plus extra for drizzling
- 2 tablespoons white chocolate, chopped
- handful of raspberries
- ½ apple, cored and finely chopped
- 1¼ cups (300ml) coconut milk

Mix all the ingredients in a large bowl and chill overnight in the refrigerator. Serve drizzled with extra maple syrup.

Choccy Avocado Pots Creamy, smooth, and perfect for a quick dessert.

SERVES 4

– 1 teaspoon vanilla extract
– 4 tablespoons coconut milk
– 2 tablespoons maple syrup
– ⅓ cup + 2 tablespoons
  (125g) semi-sweet
  chocolate, melted
  (see page 20)
– pinch of salt
– 2 ripe avocados,
  peeled and stoned
– grated chocolate,
  to decorate

Mix the vanilla, coconut milk, and maple syrup with the melted chocolate and transfer to a blender. Add the salt and avocado, and blitz until the mixture is smooth and creamy. Divide between four glasses or coffee cups and chill in the refrigerator until ready to serve, sprinkled with grated chocolate.

Rocky Road
Needs no introduction—it's considered a classic for good reason.

MAKES 12 SQUARES

- 1½ cups (250g) milk chocolate, chopped
- ½ cup (100g) butter
- 1 tablespoon dark corn syrup
- 1¼ cups (150g) graham crackers, crushed
- ¾ cups (50g) mini marshmallows
- ¼ cup (50g) dried cranberries
- confectioners' sugar, to dust

Line an 8-inch (20cm) square brownie tin with nonstick parchment paper. Place the chocolate, butter, and syrup in a medium saucepan over a low heat and warm until melted, stirring to mix. Add the remaining ingredients and mix until everything is well coated in chocolate. Transfer the mixture to the prepared tin and press into an even layer using a spatula. Chill in the refrigerator for 2 hours, then cut into 12 squares and serve dusted with confectioners' sugar.

Marbled Florentine Candies

Little mouthfuls of delight bejeweled with dried fruits and nuts, ideal for serving with coffee. Use whatever shaped cutter you like, but it should be about 1¼ inches (3cm) across.

MAKES 30-40

- ⅓ cup (100g) milk chocolate, melted (see page 20)
- ⅓ cup (100g) semi-sweet chocolate, melted (see page 20)
- ⅓ cup (100g) white chocolate, melted (see page 20)
- ¼ cup (25g) shelled pistachio nuts, sliced
- 3 tablespoons pine nuts
- ¼ cup (50g) mixed dried fruit, such as cranberries and chopped apricots

You will also need:
- cookie sheet
- nonstick parchment paper

Line a shallow cookie sheet with nonstick parchment paper. Pour the semi-sweet chocolate on to the paper, followed by the milk and white chocolate, and spread them out using a spatula to create an even layer of marbled chocolate. Allow the chocolate to cool in the refrigerator, but while it is still soft, use a small cutter to press into the chocolate to make deep indentations for the candies. Press the pieces of dried fruit and nuts into the tops of the sweets. Return to the refrigerator for about 1 hour or until set, then use the cutter to press right through the chocolate to separate the sweets.

Spicy, Sweet, & Salty Bark

If you are making this for children, take care not to overdo the chili and salt, or leave them out altogether and just use the fruit.

- 1⅔ cups (500g) semi-sweet chocolate, melted (see page 20)
- handful of dried mango, finely chopped
- handful of dried cherries, finely chopped
- chili flakes, to taste
- pink sea salt, to taste

You will also need:
- cookie sheet
- nonstick parchment paper

Line a shallow cookie sheet with nonstick parchment paper. Pour the chocolate on to the paper and spread out using a spatula to create an even layer. Sprinkle the toppings over the chocolate. Allow the chocolate to cool in the refrigerator for about 1 hour or until set, then break into uneven pieces and serve with hot chocolate or coffee.

Variation

For a healthier option, try Yogurt Bark. Follow the instructions for Spicy, Sweet, & Salty Bark (above), but instead of melted chocolate use Greek yogurt. Add whatever toppings you like—sliced strawberries and mango, desiccated coconut, and grated white chocolate work well and are great with a drizzle of maple syrup. Freeze the tray for 30 minutes, then break up and enjoy!

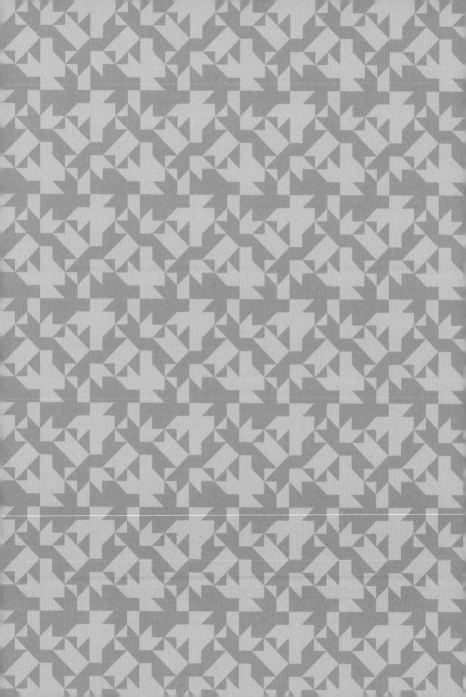

Bake

Chocolate Sugar Cookies

These cut-out cookies are good straight from the oven, but even better if you decorate them (see pages 26–7). Customize your cookies to suit any celebration—such as Christmas, Easter, or a birthday—by using festive themed cutters.

MAKES ABOUT 20

- ½ cup (125g) unsalted butter, softened
- ⅔ cup (125g) superfine sugar
- 1 egg, beaten
- 1½ cups (200g) all-purpose flour
- ¼ cup (25g) cocoa powder
- 2 tablespoons semi-sweet chocolate, melted (see page 20)

You will also need:
- plastic wrap
- 2 cookie sheets
- nonstick parchment paper

Preheat the oven to 350°F and line two cookie sheets with nonstick parchment paper.

Cream together the butter and sugar in a mixing bowl until fluffy. Add the egg and mix well, then sieve in the flour and cocoa powder. Finally add the melted chocolate and mix to form a soft dough. Wrap the dough in plastic wrap and chill in the refrigerator for 30 minutes.

Lightly dust a surface with flour and roll out the dough to ⅛ inch (2.5mm) thick. Cut out cookies with your chosen cutters and transfer to the prepared cookie sheets. Bake for 15 minutes or until crisp then allow the cookies to cool before decorating them.

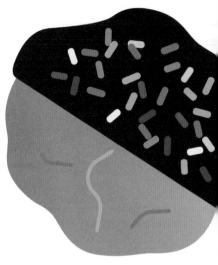

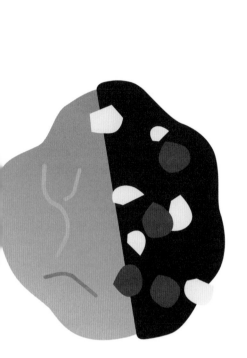

Cookie tips

- Any excess dough can be wrapped in plastic wrap and frozen for a later date.

- To make rolling out easier, divide the dough in half and roll out each half separately.

- A simple and effective way to decorate the cookies is by drizzling melted white chocolate over them using a spoon to make a scribble pattern.

White Chocolate & Rose Cookies

A hint of rosewater makes these cookies fragrant and enticing. They are sweet enough without adding extra sugar. Serve with little cups of black tea.

MAKES 15

- 1⅓ cup (175g) self-rising flour
- ½ teaspoon baking powder
- ⅓ cup (75g) unsalted butter, melted
- 1 egg, beaten
- ⅔ cup (200g) white chocolate, melted (see page 20), plus extra for drizzling
- 2 teaspoons rosewater
- crushed dried rose petals, to decorate (optional)

You will also need:
- 2 cookie sheets
- nonstick parchment paper

Preheat the oven to 350°F and line two cookie sheets with nonstick parchment paper.

Sieve the flour and baking powder into a mixing bowl, make a well in the center, add all the wet ingredients, and mix well. Use a dessertspoon to arrange 15 well-spaced mounds of the cookie batter on the prepared trays and flatten them slightly.

Bake the cookies for about 15 minutes or until they have a pale, cakey center and crispy, golden edges. Allow the cookies to cool, then transfer to a wire rack. Drizzle with white chocolate and top with rose petals, if you like. Allow the chocolate to set then store in an airtight container.

The Classic Choc Chip
This is a much-loved favorite across the world and particularly good when eaten warm from the oven.

MAKES 15

– ½ cup + 1 tablespoon (125g) butter, softened
– ⅔ cup (125g) brown sugar
– ½ teaspoon vanilla extract
– 1 egg, beaten
– ½ teaspoon baking soda
– 1¼ cups (150g) all-purpose flour, sieved
– ¾ cups + 2 tablespoons (150g) milk chocolate, chopped

You will also need:
– plastic wrap
– 2 cookie sheets
– nonstick parchment paper

Cream together the butter and sugar in a mixing bowl until fluffy. Add the vanilla and egg and mix well. Mix the bicarbonate of soda with the flour, then add to the bowl a spoonful at a time, stirring to combine. Finally add the chocolate and mix to form a sticky dough. Wrap the dough in plastic wrap and chill in the refrigerator for 1 hour.

Preheat the oven to 350°F and line two cookie sheets with nonstick parchment paper. Use a dessertspoon to arrange 15 well-spaced mounds of the cookie batter on the prepared trays. Bake the cookies for about 10 minutes or until they are soft in the center and golden at the edges. Scoff warm from the oven or allow to cool and store in an airtight container.

Chocolate Crisp Cookies These crispy
cookie bites spread and firm up in the oven.

MAKES 15-20

- ½ cup + 1 tablespoon
  (125g) butter
- ⅓ cup + 1 tablespoon
  (75g) superfine sugar
- ½ teaspoon vanilla extract
- 1 cup (125g)
  self-rising flour
- ⅓ cup (50g) milk
  chocolate, chopped
- 1 egg, beaten
- 4 tablespoons cornflakes,
  finely crushed

You will also need:
- 2 cookie sheets
- nonstick parchment paper

Preheat the oven to 350°F and line two cookie
sheets with nonstick parchment paper.

Cream together the butter, sugar, and vanilla
in a mixing bowl until fluffy. Sieve the flour in
a little at a time and mix well, then add the
chocolate, followed by the egg. The mixture
will be quite sticky.

Use damp hands to roll the mixture into
walnut-sized balls. Toss the balls in the crushed
cornflakes then flatten them slightly and arrange
them well spaced on the prepared cookie sheets.
Bake for 15 minutes or until crisp and golden.
Allow to cool then store in an airtight container.

Chocolate Flapjacks
An oldie but a goody, and one of the most satisfying snacks.

MAKES 16

- ⅔ cup (150g) butter, plus extra for greasing
- 1 tablespoon dark corn syrup
- ¾ cup (150g) brown sugar
- 2½ cups (200g) rolled oats
- ⅓ cup (50g) semi-sweet chocolate, chopped
- 1 teaspoon ground cinnamon
- melted white chocolate (see page 20), to decorate

You will also need:
- 9-inch (23cm) square baking pan

Preheat the oven to 350°F and grease a square baking pan.

Melt the butter in a large saucepan, add the dark corn syrup and sugar, and stir well. Add the oats, chocolate, and cinnamon and stir again until well combined.

Spoon the mixture into the prepared pan and spread out to form an even layer. Bake for about 30 minutes, or until golden and crisp round the edges. Cut into 16 pieces in the pan while still warm, then set aside to cool. Drizzle the cooled flapjacks with white chocolate, allow to set, then divide into bars and store in an airtight container.

Flapjack flavor combos

Instead of mixing chopped semi-sweet chocolate and cinnamon into the flapjack mixture, try these other winning combinations:

- 2 tablespoons chopped white chocolate and a handful of finely chopped dried mango.

- 2 tablespoons chopped milk chocolate and a handful of finely chopped hazelnuts.

- ⅓ cup (50g) chopped semi-sweet chocolate and 1 dessertspoon of finely diced stem ginger with a teaspoon of syrup from the jar.

Semi-sweet Chocolate & Ginger Mug Cake
Deliciously rich and warming, yet not too sweet, this is a quick and easy chocolate fix.

SERVES 1

- 2 tablespoons all-purpose flour
- 1 tablespoon superfine sugar
- ¼ teaspoon baking powder
- 2 teaspoons ground ginger
- 2 tablespoons semi-sweet chocolate, chopped
- 1 small egg
- 2 tablespoons milk
- 1 tablespoon olive oil

Mix all the dry ingredients together in a large mug then add the wet ingredients one at a time, mixing in between.

Place in the microwave and set it to medium power (about 600W). Cook for about 1 minute 20 seconds until the cake has risen and bounces back when pressed. Continue to cook in 10-second bursts if it's not quite done. Allow to cool for 1 minute before tucking in.

White Chocolate & Banana Mug Cake

Scrumptious, moist, and made in minutes, just right for when you need a sweet pick-me-up.

SERVES 1

– 2 tablespoons
  all-purpose flour
– 1 dessertspoon
  brown sugar
– ¼ teaspoon
  baking powder
– 2 tablespoons milk
– 1 tablespoon olive oil
– 1 small egg
– ⅓ ripe banana, mashed
– 1 tablespoon white
  chocolate, chopped

Mix all the dry ingredients in a large mug, add the milk, oil, and egg one at a time, mixing in between, then add the banana and chocolate and mix again.

Place in the microwave and set it to medium power (about 600W). Cook for about 1 minute 20 seconds until the cake has risen and bounces back when pressed. Continue to cook in 10-second bursts if it's not quite done. Allow to cool for 1 minute before tucking in.

Pecan Blondies
Deliciously chocolaty and golden—crispy on the outside, soft in the center, and studded with crunchy pecans.

MAKES 16

- 2 cups (350g) white chocolate, chopped
- ⅓ cup (75g) butter
- 3 eggs
- ⅔ cup (125g) superfine sugar
- 1 teaspoon vanilla extract
- 1¼ cup (150g) self-rising flour
- ¾ cup (100g) pecan nuts, chopped

You will also need:
- 9-inch (23cm) square baking pan
- nonstick parchment paper

Preheat the oven to 350°F and line a square baking pan with nonstick parchment paper.

Melt one-third of the chocolate with the butter in a small saucepan over a low heat, stirring until smooth. Whisk the eggs, sugar, and vanilla together in a large bowl until frothy, then add the melted chocolate mixture and stir. Sieve in the flour a little at a time and mix until well combined. Add the remaining chopped chocolate and pecans and stir well.

Transfer the blondie mixture to the tin and bake for 30 minutes, or until golden and coming away from the edges. The blondies should remain moist and fudgy in the center. Once cooled, cut into 16 squares and store in an airtight container.

Mocha Brownies Rich and fudgy—they will literally melt in your mouth.

MAKES 16

– 1 cup + 2 tablespoons (200g) semi-sweet chocolate, chopped
– ¾ cup (175g) butter
– 2 tablespoons instant espresso powder
– 3 eggs
– 1 cup (200g) superfine sugar
– 1 teaspoon vanilla extract
– 1 tablespoon maple syrup
– ¾ cup (100g) self-rising flour
– 1 cup + 2 tablespoons (200g) milk chocolate, chopped

Preheat the oven to 350°F and line a 9-inch (23cm) square baking pan with nonstick parchment paper. Melt the chocolate with the butter in a small saucepan over a low heat, stirring until smooth, then add the coffee. Whisk the eggs and sugar together in a large bowl until frothy, then add the melted chocolate mixture, vanilla, and maple syrup and stir. Sieve in the flour a little at a time and mix until well combined. Add the chopped milk chocolate and stir well. Transfer the brownie mixture to the pan and bake for 30 minutes, or until crisp on the outside but soft and fudgy in the center. Plunge the base of the pan into cold water to stop the cooking, taking care not to get the brownies wet, then cool fully in the pan. Cut into 16 squares and store in an airtight container.

Brownie tips

Brownies should have a crisp top and edges, but be moist and gooey in the center. Try these tips to achieve brownie perfection.

- Use good-quality ingredients.
- Beat the eggs and sugar well to get plenty of air into them.
- Don't overbake the brownies as they will become dry. Keep a close eye during the final minutes of baking.
- Give the bottom of the pan a cold bath when it comes out of the oven to stop the brownies cooking further and they will be nice and fudgy.
- Allow the brownies to cool fully in the pan before attempting to cut and eat them.

Milk Chocolate Cupcakes

Topped with white chocolate buttercream, these double-chocolate delights are great for parties or a thoughtful birthday gift.

MAKES 12

- ½ cup + 1 tablespoon (125g) unsalted butter, softened
- ⅔ cup (125g) superfine sugar
- 1 tablespoon cocoa powder
- 1 cup (125g) self-rising flour
- 2 large eggs, beaten
- 2 tablespoons milk chocolate, melted (see page 20)
- White Chocolate Buttercream (see page 19), for topping
- grated chocolate, to decorate

You will also need:
- 12-hole cupcake tray
- paper baking cups
- pastry bag fitted with a rosette nozzle

Preheat the oven to 350°F and line a cupcake tray with baking cups.

Cream the butter and sugar together in a mixing bowl until fluffy. Mix the cocoa with the flour, then sieve a little of the mixture into the bowl, stirring between additions and alternating with a little of the beaten egg, until both are used up. Add the melted chocolate and mix well, then add a splash of boiling water to make the batter glossy.

Divide the mixture between the baking cups and bake for approximately 15 minutes until a knife inserted into one of the cakes comes out clean. Cool the cakes on a wire rack, then pipe a rosette of buttercream on top of each. Add a sprinkling of grated chocolate to decorate. Store in an airtight container.

Vegan Chocolate Muffins Moist, rich, and filling, and a breeze to make.

- 1½ cups (200g) all-purpose flour
- 2 teaspoons baking powder
- pinch of salt
- ¼ cup (25g) cocoa powder
- ½ cup (100g) superfine sugar
- 2¾ tablespoons light olive oil
- ¾ cup + 2 tablespoons (200ml) water
- 2 tablespoons vegan milk chocolate, finely chopped

You will also need:
- 8-hole muffin tray
- paper baking cups

Preheat the oven to 350°F and line a muffin tray with baking cups.

Sieve the flour, baking powder, salt, and cocoa into a mixing bowl, add the sugar, and gently mix to combine. Add the oil and water, mix until just combined, then gently fold in the chocolate, taking care not to overmix.

Divide the mixture between the eight cups and bake for 20 minutes or until dark golden brown and bouncy to the touch. Allow to cool then store in an airtight container.

White Chocolate & Mango Muffins

Slightly bready and not too sweet. If you don't have mango, use fresh berries instead.

MAKES 12

– 2⅓ cups (300g)
self-rising flour
– ¾ cup + 1 tablespoon
(165g) superfine sugar
– 1 large egg
– 4 teaspoons vegetable oil
– 1 cup (240ml) whole milk
– ¾ cup (125g) ripe mango,
finely chopped
– ⅓ cup (100g) white
chocolate, finely chopped

You will also need:
– 12-hole muffin tray
– paper baking cups

Preheat the oven to 350°F and line a muffin tray with baking cups.

Sieve the flour into a mixing bowl, add the sugar, and gently mix to combine. Whisk the egg, oil, and milk together in a jug then add to the mixing bowl and mix until just combined. Gently fold in the mango and chocolate, taking care not to overmix.

Divide the mixture between the 12 cups and bake for 20–25 minutes or until golden and bouncy to the touch. Allow to cool then store in an airtight container.

Chocolate Banana Bread

For maximum enjoyment, eat this loaf while still warm—it is absolutely delicious and will disappear in no time! This needs no accompaniment and is a great way to use up any brown bananas languishing in the fruit bowl.

MAKES 1 SMALL LOAF

- ½ cup + 1 tablespoon (125g) butter, softened, plus extra for greasing
- ⅓ cup + 1 tablespoon (75g) superfine sugar
- 1 teaspoon baking powder
- 1 cup (125g) all-purpose flour
- 2 large eggs, beaten
- 1 teaspoon vanilla extract
- 2 ripe bananas, roughly mashed
- ⅓ cup (100g) milk or semi-sweet chocolate, chopped

You will also need:
- small loaf pan
- nonstick parchment paper

Preheat the oven to 350°F and line a small loaf pan with nonstick parchment paper. Cream the butter and sugar together in a mixing bowl until fluffy. Mix the baking powder with the flour, then sieve a little of the mixture into the bowl, stirring between additions and alternating with a little of the beaten egg, until both are used up. Fold in the vanilla, bananas, and chocolate, then spoon the mixture into the prepared pan and level with a spatula. Bake for 45 minutes to 1 hour, or until golden and a knife inserted into the loaf comes out clean. Eat warm or allow to cool and store in an airtight container.

Variations

There are so many delicious things you can add to banana bread—for a start, any type of chocolate will work really well. You could combine ⅓ cup (100g) of white chocolate with dried cranberries or blueberries, or you could stick with semi-sweet chocolate but add 2 tablespoons of rum instead of the vanilla. Chocolate and orange always works well—try semi-sweet chocolate with a measure of orange liqueur and some finely grated orange zest. Banana bread is endlessly versatile and always delicious.

Simple Chocolate Cake

So easy to make, you can't go wrong. Any time is a good time for chocolate cake.

SERVES 8-10

- 1 cup + 2 tablespoons (250g) butter, softened
- 1¼ cups (250g) superfine sugar
- 2 cups (250g) self-rising flour
- 4 large eggs, beaten
- ¼ cup (25g) cocoa powder
- ¾ cup + 2 tablespoons (200ml) whole milk
- 2 teaspoons vanilla extract
- ⅓ cup (100g) semi-sweet chocolate, melted (see page 20)
- 4 tablespoons raspberry preserves
- Milk Chocolate Buttercream (see page 19) or Fudge Frosting (see page 101), for decorating

You will also need:
- 2 x 8-inch (20cm) cake pans

Preheat the oven to 350°F and grease two cake pans.

Cream the butter and sugar together in a mixing bowl until fluffy. Sieve a little of the flour into the bowl, stirring between additions and alternating with a little of the beaten egg, until both are used up.

Mix the cocoa powder, milk, and vanilla with the melted chocolate in a jug, add to the cake batter, and gently fold in. Divide the mixture between the cake pans and level with a spatula. Bake for about 20 minutes, or until a knife inserted into the cakes comes out clean. Transfer the cakes to a wire rack to cool.

Sandwich the cakes together with the raspberry preserves and one-quarter of the buttercream or frosting, then decorate with the remaining buttercream or frosting.

Fudge Frosting

Beat 2 cups (250g) confectioners' sugar with 1 cup + 2 tablespoons (250g) softened butter until creamy, then add ¾ cup (250g) melted and cooled semi-sweet chocolate. This will be enough to completely cover an 8-inch (20cm) cake.

Squidgy Beer Desserts
These individual desserts have a firm crusty top hiding a gooey fudgy center. Serve with vanilla ice cream or cream.

SERVES 4

- ⅓ cup (100g) milk chocolate, chopped
- ¼ cup (50g) butter, plus extra for greasing
- 3 tablespoons cocoa powder
- ⅓ cup (75g) brown sugar
- 2 eggs, separated
- 1 teaspoon vanilla extract
- 4 tablespoons half and half
- 2 tablespoons dry stout or dark beer

You will also need:
- 4 small oven-safe dishes

Preheat the oven to 325°F and grease four small oven-safe dishes with butter.

Put the chocolate and butter in a mixing bowl and melt slowly in a microwave on a low-medium setting (see page 20), checking and stirring every few seconds. Allow to cool a little, then add the cocoa powder, two-thirds of the sugar, the egg yolks, vanilla, half and half, and stout or beer and mix together until smooth.

In a separate bowl, whisk the egg whites until soft peaks form, then slowly add the remaining sugar, a little at a time, whisking until you have a meringue-like consistency. Gently fold the egg whites into the chocolate batter, taking care not to knock out too much of the air.

Divide the mixture between the prepared dishes and bake for 8–10 minutes until just firm and crisp on top, but moist and saucy underneath. Serve immediately.

Roasted Bananas with Chocolate Sauce

If you have any overripe bananas in your fruit bowl, don't throw them away. Peel them, cut in half lengthways, and arrange in an oven-safe dish. Dot with butter and roast at 350°F for about 20 minutes, or until soft and golden and sitting in juice. Serve with cream or ice cream, accompanied by one of the sauces on pages 12–15.

Chocolate Orange Sheet Cake

This is a lovely moist cake that can be made with or without orange drizzle. It will stay fresh for up to two weeks, but is unlikely to last that long.

SERVES 12

- 1 cup + 2 tablespoons (250g) butter, softened
- 1¼ cups (250g) superfine sugar
- 2 cups (250g) self-rising flour
- 4 large eggs, beaten
- finely grated zest and juice of 1 orange
- 1 tablespoon orange liqueur
- 1 cup (175g) milk chocolate, chopped

You will also need:
- 9-inch (23cm) square baking pan
- nonstick parchment paper

Preheat the oven to 350°F and line a square baking pan with nonstick parchment paper.

Cream the butter and sugar together in a mixing bowl until fluffy. Sieve a little of the flour into the bowl, stirring between additions and alternating with a little of the beaten egg, until both are used up. Mix in the orange zest, juice, and liqueur, then fold in the chocolate.

Transfer mixture to the prepared pan and level with a spatula. Bake for 25–30 minutes, or until golden and a knife inserted into the cake comes out clean.

If you would like to add the orange drizzle topping, allow the cake to cool for 20–30 minutes then use a skewer to make small holes all over the cake. Pour the drizzle evenly over the cake and leave to cool completely in the pan. Store in an airtight container for up to two weeks.

Orange drizzle

Gently warm the juice of half an orange with the juice of half a lemon in a small saucepan. Add ½ cup (100g) superfine sugar and stir over a low heat until the sugar has dissolved.

White Chocolate Meringues
These crisp meringues are soft and chewy inside and topped with nuts and white chocolate.

MAKES 8

- 4 egg whites
- 1¼ cups (225g) superfine sugar
- 1 teaspoon vanilla extract
- ⅔ cup (200g) white chocolate, melted (see page 18)
- chopped pistachio nuts, for decorating

You will also need:
- large cookie sheet
- nonstick parchment paper

Preheat the oven to 300°F and line the cookie sheet with nonstick parchment paper.

Whisk the egg whites in a mixing bowl with an electric whisk on low speed until bubbly, then increase the speed to medium for 1 minute. Whisk on full speed until soft peaks form, then add the sugar a tablespoon at a time, continuing to whisk on full speed. Add the vanilla and whisk again until the meringue is glossy and forms soft peaks.

Arrange eight large mounds of meringue on the cookie sheet and place in the oven. Immediately reduce the temperature to 275°F and bake for 1 hour then turn off the heat, but leave the meringues in the oven until they are completely cool. They should be crispy on the outside and soft and chewy on the inside. Drizzle the meringues with the white chocolate and sprinkle with the pistachios. Allow the chocolate to set and store in an airtight container.

The Many Faces of Chocolate

Gone are the days when there were just three types of chocolate. Nowadays we are spoilt for choice with so many variations and flavors. Chocolate is classified by the proportion of cocoa to fat in the bar, but the taste varies according to where the cocoa beans were grown and how they were fermented— it has little to do with how the chocolate was made.

Raw chocolate is chocolate that hasn't been mixed with any other ingredients—it hasn't been processed or heated. It is mainly found in regions that grow chocolate, and consumers outside these areas tend to find it less palatable than its sweeter cousins. It is promoted as being healthier as it has no sugar or fat added and is said to protect the nervous system and reduce blood pressure and the risk of stroke. It also contains many vitamins and minerals, including magnesium and calcium.

Semi-sweet chocolate or plain chocolate is a mixture of cocoa solids and cocoa butter, without any milk. It has a higher percentage of cocoa solids than milk chocolate, ranging from 50% to 100%. The higher the percentage, the more bitter the taste. Semi-sweet chocolate can be eaten by itself or added to recipes to give depth of flavor. If you consume high-percentage semi-sweet chocolate in moderation, there are all sorts of health benefits, including improved blood flow and brain function, lower cholesterol, and a reduced risk of heart disease. Semi-sweet chocolate tends to be more brittle and to snap when broken, because it isn't softened by the addition of dairy products.

Milk chocolate contains powdered milk, condensed milk, or liquid milk and sugar. The first milk chocolate bar appeared in Switzerland in the 1860s when the Nestlé company began working with a chocolatier named Daniel Peter. Milk chocolate is not considered to be as beneficial to health, as the nutrients are outweighed by the added fat and sugar. Milk chocolate has a softer texture due to the added dairy.

White chocolate is the softest and sweetest chocolate, made from sugar, milk, and cocoa butter, with no cocoa solids at all. It has little benefit in health terms, but makes a delicious treat if you aren't a fan of the darker chocolates. White chocolate was first launched in Europe in 1936, also by Nestlé.

Ruby chocolate is a relative newcomer to the chocolate market. It was developed in 2004 and released to market in 2017. Made from the ruby cocoa bean, it is mainly grown in Ecuador, Brazil, and the Ivory Coast. Characterized by its distinctive pink-red color and its fruity, sour but smooth taste, ruby chocolate was developed in Belgium and contains about 47% cocoa solids. It is less rich than milk chocolate as the beans are not fermented.

Twist

Chili with Chocolate
Adding a few squares of chocolate to your favorite chili recipe is a sure-fire way to make it extra tasty and glossy, with a greater depth of flavor.

SERVES 4

- 1 tablespoon olive oil
- 1 large onion, chopped
- 1 red bell pepper, chopped
- 2 garlic cloves, chopped
- 1 fresh red chili, seeded and finely chopped
- 1–2 teaspoons chili powder
- 1 teaspoon smoked paprika
- 2 cups (500g) ground beef
- ⅔ cup (150ml) beef broth
- 1 can (14 ounces / 400g) diced tomatoes
- 2 tablespoons tomato purée
- 1 can (14 ounces / 400g) black beans or kidney beans, rinsed
- 2 tablespoons semi-sweet chocolate, chopped
- salt and pepper, to taste

To serve:
- rice or tortillas
- sour cream
- guacamole
- grated cheese

Heat the oil in a large saucepan over a medium heat, add the onion, bell pepper, garlic, and fresh chili, and cook, stirring, until softened. Add the chili powder and paprika and stir. Add the ground beef, breaking it up with a spoon. Turn up the heat and brown the meat, then add the broth, tomatoes, and purée. Add the beans and bring to the boil, then reduce the heat to a simmer and cook for 20–30 minutes or until rich and thick. Add the chocolate and stir in, then season to taste with salt and pepper. Serve with rice or tortillas, sour cream, guacamole, and grated cheese.

Chicken Mole
A Mexican speciality that is spicy and nutty with a subtle flavor of chocolate.

SERVES 4

– 1-2 tablespoons olive oil
– 1 large onion, chopped
– 2 fresh red chilies, seeded and finely chopped
– 3 garlic cloves, chopped
– 1 teaspoon ground cumin
– 1 teaspoon ground cinnamon
– 8 boneless, skinless chicken thighs
– 1 can (14 ounces/400g) chopped tomatoes
– 2 teaspoons chipotle paste
– 2 tablespoons peanut butter
– ⅓ cup (50g) raisins
– 1½ tablespoons semi-sweet chocolate, chopped
– salt and pepper, to taste

To serve:
– handful of chopped cilantro
– lime wedges
– sour cream
– rice

Heat 1 tablespoon of the oil in a saucepan over a low heat, add the onion and cook until golden and softened. Add the chilies and garlic and cook for 30 seconds before adding the cumin and cinnamon. Turn up the heat, add the chicken and a little more oil, if needed, and brown the chicken on all sides.

Add the tomatoes and chipotle paste and bring to the boil. Reduce the heat to a simmer, stir, and add the peanut butter. Cook on a low heat for 30 minutes, then add the raisins and chocolate, stir, and cook for another 10 minutes. Season to taste with salt and pepper and serve with fresh cilantro, lime wedges, sour cream, and rice.

Posh Liver & Bacon

This recipe is based on an Italian sauce called *agrodolce*, meaning "sour and sweet." The dish originated in Sicily and has a long history, dating back to 965.

SERVES 4

- ¼ cup (50g) butter
- 2 red onions, chopped
- 1 fresh red chili, seeded and finely chopped
- ½ cup (125g) pancetta, diced
- 1 tablespoon olive oil
- 1 cup (200g) chicken livers, patted dry and dusted with flour
- 3 tablespoons balsamic vinegar
- 1½ tablespoons semi-sweet chocolate, chopped
- 4 slices of white crusty bread, toasted and buttered

Melt half the butter in a large skillet over a low heat, add the onions and chili, and cook until golden and softened. Remove from the skillet and set aside. Turn up the heat, add the pancetta to the skillet, and cook until crispy. Remove from the skillet and set aside with the onions.

Add the remaining butter and the olive oil to the skillet and cook the livers for 3–4 minutes, turning from time to time, until golden all over. Return the onion and pancetta to the skillet and add the vinegar and semi-sweet chocolate. Stir well, reduce the heat, and cook gently for 10 minutes to melt the chocolate to a glossy sauce. Serve on the toast.

All-Day Breakfast with a Twist

Breakfast favorites like you've never had them before!

SERVES 2

- 2 rashers of Canadian bacon, cooked and roughly chopped
- 1 can (14 ounces/400g) baked beans in tomato sauce
- 1 tablespoon semi-sweet chocolate, chopped
- 2 large slices of bread, toasted and buttered
- grated cheese, for sprinkling

Place the bacon, beans, and chocolate in a saucepan over a gentle heat and cook, stirring, until bubbling. Pour over the toast and top with grated cheese.

Easy *Pain au Chocolat*

This great breakfast hack is quite simply chocolate on toast, either melted or chopped. If you have a baguette to hand, do it the French way—chunks of semi-sweet chocolate inside a wedge of crusty baguette.

French Toast *au Chocolat*

An indulgent white chocolate center makes this the breakfast of dreams.

- 4 slices of white bread, buttered
- 2 tablespoons white chocolate, melted (see page 20)
- 2 eggs
- 1 tablespoon heavy cream
- 1 tablespoon maple syrup
- 2 tablespoons butter

To serve:
- ground cinnamon
- confectioners' sugar

Lay two slices of the bread on a board, buttered sides up, and spread with the melted chocolate, not quite to the edges. Cover with the other two slices of bread, buttered sides down, to make two sandwiches and press to seal.

Whisk the eggs with the cream and maple syrup in a wide bowl. Melt half the butter in a skillet over a medium heat until hot but not smoking. Coat both sides of one of the sandwiches in the egg mixture then cook in the skillet for about 1 minute on each side, or until golden brown. Repeat with the second sandwich. Cut the sandwiches in half, dust with cinnamon and confectioners' sugar, and serve immediately.

Sweet Toastie fillings

- Banana and grated chocolate
- Cream cheese, pear, and melted chocolate
- Brie, chocolate, and cranberry sauce
- Ricotta, fig, and white chocolate

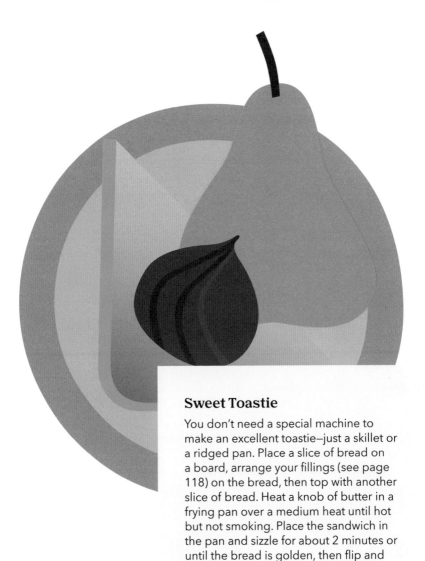

Sweet Toastie

You don't need a special machine to make an excellent toastie—just a skillet or a ridged pan. Place a slice of bread on a board, arrange your fillings (see page 118) on the bread, then top with another slice of bread. Heat a knob of butter in a frying pan over a medium heat until hot but not smoking. Place the sandwich in the pan and sizzle for about 2 minutes or until the bread is golden, then flip and repeat on the other side until the filling has melted.

Herby Mushroom Pasta with Chocolate

Mushrooms, cream, and semi-sweet chocolate taste surprisingly good together.

SERVES 4

- 3 cups (350g) dried linguine
- ¼ cup (50g) butter
- dash of olive oil
- 4 cups (300g) mushrooms, sliced
- 4 shallots, diced
- ⅔ cup (150ml) heavy cream
- ⅓ cup (75ml) white wine
- 4–5 thyme sprigs or a few sage leaves, chopped
- salt and pepper

To serve:
- grated semi-sweet chocolate
- grated Parmesan cheese

Cook the pasta according to the packet instructions. Melt the butter and oil in a large skillet over a medium heat and cook the mushrooms and shallots until softened and cooked through.

Add the cream, wine, and herbs, stir well, and season with salt and pepper. Heat through, then add the cooked pasta and toss with the sauce. Serve topped with grated semi-sweet chocolate and Parmesan.

Goat's Cheese & White Chocolate Risotto

This delicious dish is rich and creamy.

SERVES 4-6

- 2 tablespoons olive oil
- 1 onion, chopped
- 1 garlic clove, chopped
- 1⅓ cups (300g) risotto rice
- 1¼ cups (300ml) white wine
- 3 cups (700ml) hot vegetable or chicken broth
- 1 sweet potato, cubed and steamed until tender
- 4 thyme sprigs, stalks removed
- 1¼ cups (125g) goat's cheese
- 1 tablespoon white chocolate, chopped
- salt and pepper

Heat the oil in a large saucepan over a low heat and fry the onion until softened. Add the garlic and fry for another minute. Turn up the heat to medium, add the rice, stir until coated in the oil, then add the wine. Keep stirring, add a ladleful of the hot broth, and stir until it has been absorbed by the rice. Continue cooking and stirring and adding more broth for 10 minutes.

Stir in the sweet potato cubes, the thyme, and salt and pepper to taste. Continue cooking, stirring, and adding stock until the risotto is creamy and the rice is tender with a slight bite to it. Just before serving, add the cheese and chocolate and gently stir through so that they melt into the rice. Serve immediately.

Quick & Easy Sweet & Salty Snacks

These snacks have been given a chocolaty twist to make them far from ordinary. They might just become addictive.

Crispy bacon treats
Broil a few rashers of Canadian bacon until crispy and allow to cool on a paper towel. Dip the rashers in melted semi-sweet chocolate and leave to set on a wire rack.

Popcorn
Make a bowl of salted popcorn following the package instructions, or buy a bag of ready-made salted popcorn. Spread the popcorn out on a cookie sheet lined with parchment paper and drizzle with the melted chocolate of your choice.

Salted cashews
Drizzle melted milk or semi-sweet chocolate over a bowl of salty cashew nuts for an unexpectedly delicious treat.

Chili chips with chocolate dip
Pour a bag of chili-flavored potato chips into a bowl and serve with a small bowl of melted semi-sweet chocolate for dipping. Your friends might pull a face at first, but once they try them they will be converted!

Cherry tomato lollies
Spear cherry tomatoes on toothpicks and dip into melted milk chocolate and then into a bowl of chopped nuts. Allow them to cool and harden, then insert the bottoms of the toothpicks into a grapefruit to serve.

Really Great Gravy

Take the cooked meat out of the roasting pan and set aside. Place the pan on the stovetop over a medium heat. Add a little flour to the meat juices in the pan and stir well to make a paste. Stir in a glass of red wine and some hot beef broth to create a smooth gravy and bring up to a bubble. Cook gently for 5 minutes, then add two or three squares of semi-sweet chocolate. Season to taste and stir well until the chocolate melts and the gravy is rich and glossy.

How to Make Chocolate
Making chocolate at home is easier than you might think and can be done with just a few ingredients.

Semi-sweet chocolate:
- ⅔ cup (140g) cocoa butter
- 1 cup (100g) cocoa powder
- 2 tablespoons maple syrup

Milk chocolate:
- ⅔ cup (140g) cocoa butter
- ¾ cup (80g) cocoa powder
- 1 cup (100g) confectioners' sugar
- ⅓ cup (30g) milk powder

White chocolate:
- ½ cup (100g) cocoa butter
- 1 cup (100g) confectioners' sugar
- ⅔ cup (60g) milk powder

You will also need:
- silicone chocolate mold

Melt the cocoa butter in a bain marie (see page 20). Mix the dry ingredients together in a bowl, then sieve them a little at a time into the bowl with the melted cocoa butter and stir well to mix. Take the chocolate off the heat and continue stirring until smooth and glossy. Pour the chocolate into a silicone mold and allow to cool in the refrigerator for about 1 hour until set.

Index

About the Author & Illustrator

Sarah Ford has written many giftable bestsellers, including *50 Ways to Kill a Slug*, *What Would Unicorn Do?*, *Be a Flamingo*, *The Chinese Zodiac*, and *It's the Little Things*.

Kari Modén, who created the unique illustrations, has a stellar client list including Bonnier Fakta, *Cosmopolitan*, *Die Zeit*, Dorling Kindersley, *Elle*, *GQ*, *Tatler*, *The Guardian*, *The New Yorker*, and *The New York Times*.